W9-CSB-564

Sheila Anderson

Lerner Publications Company
Minneapolis

To Abigail Chiaokhiao

Lerner Publications Company
A division of Lerner Publishing Group, Inc.
241 First Avenue North
Minneapolis, MN 55401 U.S.A.

Website address: www.lernerbooks.com

Library of Congress Cataloging-in-Publication Data

Anderson, Sheila.
Are You Ready for Fall? / by Sheila M. Anderson.
p. cm. — (Lightning bolt books™ – Our four seasons)
Includes index.
ISBN 978-0-7613-4586-2 (lib. bdg. : alk. paper)
1. Autumn —Juvenile literature. I. Title.
QB637.7.A53 2010
508.2—dc22 2009016408

Manufactured in the United States of America
1 – BP – 12/15/09

Contents

Sights and Sounds of Fall

Crunch! Crunch! What is making that sound?

Someone is walking through crisp, dry leaves.

Squirrels hop about, swishing their bushy tails. They gather smooth, brown acorns. Their cheeks are puffed up like popcorn balls.

Squirrels collect acorns and hide them in tree trunks.

Leaves on trees turn bright yellow, flame orange, and vibrant red. They glow in the bright sunlight.

This sunflower has turned dry and brown.

Grass turns yellow. Plants and flowers turn brown and shrivel on their stems and branches.

Fall Weather

Wind whooshes through the trees. Dead leaves float and spiral as they blow to the ground.

Dead leaves blow into a pond.

Time to rake!

Let's make a pile of leaves to play in.

The air is getting cool. People put on warm sweaters and long pants when they go outdoors. Better zip up your jacket!

The air is dry. A chilly breeze blows my hair.

Be sure to wear a sweater on a cool fall day.

An icy layer of white frost coats the grass and leaves on the ground.

The frost disappears before lunchtime.

In the afternoon, it's warm enough to play outside without a heavy coat.

Fall Activities

When fall arrives, children go back to school. It is fun to see friends and favorite teachers again. I wonder who will be in my class.

A school bus rumbles to a stop.

Families pick ripe red apples at the orchard.

Let's make a pie!

People harvest vegetables from their gardens. They will store them to eat when winter comes.

This man picked squash from his garden.

Farmers harvest crops from their fields

The Fall World

Bears eat lots of berries and leaves. They grow fat enough to survive while they hibernate through the winter. They won't eat again until spring.

Other animals hide food to eat during the winter months.

Pumpkins are bright orange and plump on their vines.

Pumpkins lie in a farmer's field.

This pumpkin will make a perfect jack-o'-lantern.

People gather seeds to plant in the spring.

Seeds pop out of a milkweed plant. The wind will blow them to a new home.

Winter Is Coming

Soon, days begin to get shorter. It gets dark earlier.

The temperature begins to drop. **Can you see your breath?**

Animals grow thick winter coats.

This wolf has grown a warm, shaggy coat for the winter.

Birds begin flying south. Temperatures are warmer there.

Flocks of Canada geese fly in the shape of the letter v.

Winter is on its way.

Why Do Leaves Change Color?

Leaves get their green color from a chemical called chlorophyll. All leaves contain chlorophyll. Plants use it to make food.

Plants make food from water, sunlight, and carbon dioxide (a gas in the air). Chlorophyll helps them to do this.

When fall arrives, the chlorophyll in leaves breaks down. Then the green color in the leaves goes away. Reds, yellows, and oranges appear.

Bright reds, yellows, and oranges are in leaves all year long. But in spring and summer, chlorophyll covers them up!

Glossary

acorn: the seed of an oak tree

frost: a covering of tiny ice crystals that occurs when moisture on an object freezes

harvest: to pick or gather food

hibernate: to spend winter in a sleeplike state

jack-o'-lantern: a pumpkin with a face carved into it and a candle inside

shrivel: to dry up and wilt

temperature: how warm or cold the air is

Further Reading

Ehlert, Lois. *Leaf Man.* Orlando, Fl.: Harcourt, 2005.

Enchanted Learning: Earth's Seasons
http://www.enchantedlearning.com/subjects/astronomy/planets/earth/seasons.shtml

Glaser, Linda. *It's Fall!* Minneapolis: Millbrook Press, 2002.

Spinelli, Eileen. *I Know It's Autumn.* New York: HarperCollins, 2004.

Stein, David Ezra. *Leaves.* New York: G. P. Putnam's Sons, 2007.

Index

Photo Acknowledgments

The images in this book are used with the permission of: © iStockphoto.com/Skip O'Donnell, p. 1; © Petr Gnuskin/Dreamstime.com, p. 2; © Adam Weiss/Taxi/Getty Images, p. 4; © Georgette Douwma/Photographer's Choice/Getty Images, p. 5; © Karlene Schwartz, pp. 6, 7, 12, 20, 22, 25, 28; © Flirt/SuperStock, p. 8; © Brooke Slezak/Taxi/Getty Images, p. 9; © Donna Day/Stone/Getty Images, p. 10; © Sonya Farrell/Taxi/Getty Images, p. 11; © Christopher Robbins/Riser/Getty Images, p. 13; © Yellow Dog Productions/The Image Bank/Getty Images, p. 14; © Anne Ackerman/Taxi/Getty Images, p. 15; © Gwehndolehne/Dreamstime.com, p. 16; © age fotostock/SuperStock, pp. 17, 23; © iStockphoto.com/Cory Johnson, p. 18; © Prisma/SuperStock, p. 19; © Gerry Lemmo, pp. 21, 26, 30; © iStockphoto.com/Paul Kline, p. 24; © Andrew Olney/OJO Images/Getty Images, p. 27; © Richard Price/Photographer's Choice/Getty Images, p. 29; © Ariel Skelley/Blend Images/Getty Images, p. 31.

Front cover: © Elena Elisseeva/Dreamstime.com (top left); © iStockphoto.com/Ekaterina Fribus (top middle); © iStockphoto.com/Olivier Blondeau (top right); © Johner/Johner Images/Getty Images (bottom).